WORSHIP

HIS LOVE
ENDURES FOREVER

SUNDEE
TUCKER
FRAZIER

8 STUDIES
FOR INDIVIDUALS
OR GROUPS

Life
Builder
Study

INTER-VARSITY PRESS
36 Causton Street, London SW1P 4ST, England
Email: ivp@ivpbooks.com
Website: www.ivpbooks.com

Originally published in the United States of America in the LifeGuide® Bible Studies series in 2004 by InterVarsity Press, Downers Grove, Illinois
First published in Great Britain by Scripture Union in 2012
This edition published in Great Britain by Inter-Varsity Press 2019

British Library Cataloguing-in-Publication Data
A catalogue record for this book is available from the British Library.

ISBN: 978–1–78359–851–9

Printed in Great Britain by Ashford Colour Ltd, Gosport, Hampshire

Inter-Varsity Press publishes Christian books that are true to the Bible and that communicate the gospel, develop discipleship and strengthen the church for its mission in the world.

IVP originated within the Inter-Varsity Fellowship, now the Universities and Colleges Christian Fellowship, a student movement connecting Christian Unions in universities and colleges throughout Great Britain, and a member movement of the International Fellowship of Evangelical Students. Website: www.uccf.org.uk. That historic association is maintained, and all senior IVP staff and committee members subscribe to the UCCF Basis of Faith.

Contents

Getting the Most Out of
Worship

When we talk about worship, what do we mean? You may think of your weekly gathering with other Christians or, more specifically, singing to God—both of which are important aspects of worship. Singing is mentioned frequently throughout the Bible as a fitting way to praise God. As Eugene Peterson's version of Psalm 66 says:

> [God] converted sea to dry land;
>> travelers crossed the river on foot.
>> Now isn't that cause for a song? (*The Message*)

I love connecting with God through song, which I like to think of as heaven's vernacular. Music often lifts us to a transcendent plane, and certainly one of worship's functions is to prepare us for heaven. Singing is also universal; every culture sings, and all cultures will be represented in the eternal worship we participate in together (Revelation 7).

I once heard Thomas Avery, an ethnomusicologist with Wycliffe Bible Translators, explain how worship developed among the Canela people in Brazil. After the people received the gospel from a Wycliffe Bible translator, Thomas helped them develop worship songs in their own language and style. A Canela man came to the Bible translator with tears in his eyes and said, "You gave us the book in which God speaks to us, but your friend Tom gave us the songs in which we speak to God."

Singing gives many of us a way to communicate with God on a soul level. So, worship includes meeting with others to sing and honor and rededicate ourselves to God, but it is more. The eight studies in this guide are designed to fill out what that "more" is. Before you continue, however, here are some foundational truths about worship to lay the groundwork. I hope you will return to these again and again throughout the study.

First, worship is rooted in the character and permanence of God. Again and again throughout history, God has shown his people that he is strong and he is loving (Psalm 62:11-12): He is committed to our well-being and able to do all that he has promised. He has also made it clear that he wants a close relationship with us—on the level of intimate friendship or a good marriage. He expresses this desire in the form of covenants of love (Deuteronomy 7:9, 12) that he makes with his people. When we worship, we are foremost celebrating God's strong love, a love that does not threaten to lessen with each failure on our part but will endure throughout eternity because God has promised himself to us.

Even as a worship leader, I struggle to believe that God's love for me is permanent—that there's nothing I can do to make him love me less, or more. Thank God for his Word, which reveals *who* we worship. His Word says that he loves us with an everlasting love and continually draws us with his lovingkindness, building us up over and over so that we can join others in worshiping him (Jeremiah 31:3-4).

Second, worship is always a response to God's initiative and, at the same time, is meant to be an interaction. Worship is not only about what I give to God or what he gives to me: it's God receiving what he's worthy to receive and us receiving *more of God*. If you're someone who wants more of God, then studying and growing in worship is a perfect next step.

Many different Hebrew and Greek words are translated "worship" in our English Bibles, but the most prevalent are the Hebrew *hawah* and the Greek *proskyneo*, which both mean "to bow down." *Proskyneo* derives from the practice of bowing down to kiss the feet of someone. They connote reverence and submission. These terms are not used exclusively for the worship of God but for idol worship as well. There is nothing sacred in the words themselves; what makes worship sacred is the object of worship and the heart of the worshiper. In these studies, you will learn more about both.

Finally, worship is about letting our whole lives point to the supremacy and worth of God. How we make decisions, how we use our gifts and skills, how we relate to others, whether we truly depend on God day in and day out—these choices reveal whether we understand the heart of worship. For the point of worship is not worship but God. Whatever form it takes, worship is not an end in itself; rather, it facilitates a closer relationship with God, which, miracle of miracles, is what God wants to have with us. Worship is a gift, therefore, and the overflow of our enjoyment of God. Hopefully, these Bible studies will help you to open this gift and enjoy God the way you were made to.

Suggestions for Individual Study

1. As you begin each study, pray that God will speak to you through his Word.

2. Read the introduction to the study and respond to the personal reflection question or exercise. This is designed to help you focus on God and on the theme of the study.

3. Each study deals with a particular passage—so that you can delve into the author's meaning in that context. Read and reread the passage to be studied. The questions are written using the language of the New International Version, so you may wish to use that version of the Bible. The New Revised Standard Version is also recommended.

4. This is an inductive Bible study, designed to help you discover for yourself what Scripture is saying. The study includes three types of questions. *Observation* questions ask about the basic facts: who, what, when, where and how. *Interpretation* questions delve into the meaning of the passage. *Application* questions help you discover the implications of the text for growing in Christ. These three keys unlock the treasures of Scripture.

Write your answers to the questions in the spaces provided or in a personal journal. Writing can bring clarity and deeper understanding of yourself and of God's Word.

5. It might be good to have a Bible dictionary handy. Use it to look up any unfamiliar words, names or places.

6. Use the prayer suggestion to guide you in thanking God for what you have learned and to pray about the applications that have come to mind.

7. You may want to go on to the suggestion under "Now or Later," or you may want to use that idea for your next study.

Suggestions for Members of a Group Study

1. Come to the study prepared. Follow the suggestions for individual study mentioned above. You will find that careful preparation will greatly enrich your time spent in group discussion.

2. Be willing to participate in the discussion. The leader of your group will not be lecturing. Instead, he or she will be encouraging the members of the group to discuss what they have learned. The leader will be asking the questions that are found in this guide.

3. Stick to the topic being discussed. Your answers should be based on the verses which are the focus of the discussion and not on outside authorities such as commentaries or speakers. These studies focus on a particular passage of Scripture. Only rarely should you refer to other portions of the Bible. This allows for everyone to participate in indepth study on equal ground.

4. Be sensitive to the other members of the group. Listen attentively when they describe what they have learned. You may be surprised by their insights! Each question assumes a variety of answers. Many questions do not have "right" answers, particularly questions that aim at meaning or application. Instead the questions push us to explore the passage more thoroughly.

When possible, link what you say to the comments of others. Also, be affirming whenever you can. This will encourage some of the more hesitant members of the group to participate.

5. Be careful not to dominate the discussion. We are sometimes so eager to express our thoughts that we leave too little opportunity for others to respond. By all means participate! But allow others to also.

6. Expect God to teach you through the passage being discussed and through the other members of the group. Pray that you will have an enjoyable and profitable time together, but also that as a result of the study you will find ways that you can take action individually and/or as a group.

7. Remember that anything said in the group is considered confidential and should not be discussed outside the group unless specific permission is given to do so.

8. If you are the group leader, you will find additional suggestions at the back of the guide.

1

Soul Satisfaction

Psalm 63

All humans hunger and thirst for more than just food and water. In
other words, all humans worship. Whatever we think will satisfy our
hunger and thirst eventually becomes the object of our worship.
Many of us want to worship God and God alone, but we wonder if
God can satisfy us completely. At times we may feel unsure of his
presence or his intentions, especially when life is difficult or the
world seems dangerous and chaotic.

GROUP DISCUSSION. A popular advertising campaign for a soda drink
declared, "Obey your thirst." What recent advertisements cause you
to thirst or hunger for something you may or may not need?

PERSONAL REFLECTION. Have you moved from simply hearing about
God to seeing his power, goodness and lovingkindness for yourself?
Recall one or more times in worship when you have seen these
aspects of God.

In this study, we will learn from King David what catalyzes and sustains soul-satisfying worship. *Read Psalm 63.*

1. Tradition maintains that David wrote this psalm while fleeing Jerusalem because his son Absalom conspired against him to take over the

kingship. What do you notice about David's state as he calls on God?

What progression does he make from the beginning to the ending of his prayer?

2. Think of a time when you were this thirsty spiritually. How did you try to fill your sense of need?

3. Based on what David says in the psalm, how would you describe his relationship with and experience of God?

4. What does David know about God that helps him to worship God even in such a dire situation (note especially verses 3 and 7)?

5. David's experience of God's love directly affects his commitment to worship God, which he determines to do for the rest of his life (v. 4). In your own life, how have you seen the connection between experiencing God's love and your worship of God?

6. What experiences with God from his past might David be remembering in verse 6?

What personal experiences with God might you remember to catalyze and sustain your worship, particularly in tough times?

7. What does David realize about himself, his enemies and God as he worships?

8. Note that the word *soul* appears three times in this psalm (vv. 1, 5, 8). David says his soul thirsts, will be satisfied and clings to God. How does worshiping God satisfy David's soul?

9. How might David's reasons for worshiping influence your own?

10. Where have you been experiencing dissatisfaction in your life lately?

After studying this psalm, what will you do differently in your search for satisfaction?

Take time now to express to God any areas of dissatisfaction in your life, and ask him to fill you up. End by telling God why you worship him. Try to be as specific as David is.

Now or Later

Knowing, experiencing and remembering God's love are crucial to finding our satisfaction in God. Determine this week to notice God's better-than-life love. When you see examples of his love (in the Word, in an answered prayer, through another person, through a surprise, in nature or a piece of art) write them down and thank God for them (in other words, *worship*).

2

For Keeps

Why do we gather as Christians to worship God? What motivates us to meet, and to what end? What do our rituals—such as Scripture reading, baptism and Communion—mean? Are we just going through the motions, performing empty rituals? It may sometimes feel that way, but when we connect our corporate worship practices to the Lord's meeting with Moses and the elders of Israel on Mount Sinai, our worship can take on a whole new dimension.

GROUP DISCUSSION. Think of a relationship that is extremely significant to you. What actions do you and the other person take regularly (or what traditions do you maintain) that demonstrate or remind you of how important this relationship is?

PERSONAL REFLECTION. When you participate in corporate worship services, what helps you remember why you are there? If lately you've felt like you're simply going through the motions in worship, spend a few moments asking God to renew and deepen your relationship with him.

Biblical worship is centered on God's deliverance as demonstrated in concrete events. In the Old Testament the great saving event was the rescue of the Israelites from over four hundred years of slavery, after which God established a covenant with them. *Read Exodus 24:1-11.*

1. This passage could be divided into three parts: before the covenant is ratified, ratifying the covenant and celebrating the covenant. Throughout this passage, what actions (explicit or implicit) do you see the Lord taking?

What actions do the people (including Moses and the other leaders) take?

2. How does this scene remind you of ceremonies or events you have participated in?

3. What do you notice about the people's and Moses' response to God's words?

4. What role does the Book of the Covenant play in this meeting?

5. In Exodus 12, God instructs the Israelites to put the blood of a sacrificed lamb on their doorframes so they will be protected from the plague that kills the firstborn. Where and when is the blood sprinkled in *this* gathering, and what do you think these actions signify?

6. Where in this passage do you see parallels to our worship services?

7. Why do you think the leaders of Israel eat and drink in the presence of God after the covenant is formed (v. 11)?

8. What has God communicated to his people through this entire event?

9. How would worshiping with others be different if you entered each time believing that God had called you together to make a renewal of his vows to you and yours to him?

10. What is your favorite part of corporate worship?

How does that particular element help you to remember and celebrate God's covenant with you?

Spend some time thanking God for how he meets you in corporate worship. Pray for your worship service—that it would be a place where everyone gathered experiences a renewal of their relationship with God.

Now or Later

God's intentions for Israel were expanded to include those of us who are not Jewish but acknowledge Jesus as the One who permanently seals our relationship with God. *Read 1 Peter 2:4-12.* How does knowing you are part of a royal priesthood affect how you see yourself and your life?

3

Mercy,
Not Sacrifice

Psalm 50

What is the point of worship? The way some people talk about their worship experiences ("I didn't get anything out of that," or "The music rocked!") you'd think that worship is primarily for us. Others insist—mainly in reaction to such human-centered perceptions of worship—that worship is exclusively for God. Thankfully, God directs us to a life-giving understanding of how to truly honor him.

GROUP DISCUSSION. Describe a time recently when you were in trouble or in a difficult predicament with seemingly no way out. What did you do? How did things turn out?

PERSONAL REFLECTION. God wants each of us simply to bring ourselves to him in worship. Ask God what is something of worth that you offer that blesses his heart; take time to let him tell you.

God and Israel made a covenant in Exodus 24 and sealed it with the blood of sacrifice (Psalm 50:5). God promised to make the people his treasured possession, to protect, provide for and deliver them (Exodus 19:4-5; 23:25-33). The people, in turn, agreed to obey God's commands—the first and foremost of which is to worship God and God alone. Sacrifices continued to be an integral part of Israel's expression of their covenant commitment to the Lord. Unfortunately, this religious activity began to overshadow genuine gratitude, trust in and obedience to God—but God wouldn't simply stand by. *Read Psalm 50.*

---

1. God is cast in the role of a judge in this passage (vv. 4, 6), who summons (to send for with authority, order to appear in court) the earth and the heavens to corroborate his testimony against his people (v. 7). What does it seem is at the heart of God's concern for his people?

What have they done or not done in violation of their side of the covenant?

---

2. What is God not rebuking them for? Does this surprise you in any way?

---

3. How is God distinguished (or how does he distinguish himself) from humans in this psalm?

---

4. From what God says to the people, what does it seem has become their attitude in offering sacrifices to God?

5. What commands does God give to remedy the situation?

_____

6. Which one of these commands do you find easiest to do?

Which is the most difficult, and why?

_____

7. In verses 16-22 God addresses those who flagrantly disobey his covenant. What has allowed them to act this way and think there will be no consequences?

_____

8. How might intentional gratitude prepare a person to see God's salvation or make God's goodness more apparent (v. 23)?

_____

9. How would you characterize God after studying this psalm?

From what God has said here, what does he want for his people (including *you*)?

10. What religious or worship-related activities do you find easier to fulfill than certain vows or commitments you've made to God?

What might you do to become more genuinely grateful, obedient or dependent on God—in other words, to have a real relationship with God?

Take time now to "sacrifice thank offerings" by telling God everything you can think of for which you are grateful.

Now or Later

The underlying theme of Psalm 50 (perhaps of the entire Bible) is that God desires mercy, not sacrifice (see also Psalm 69:30-31; Hosea 6:6; Matthew 9:13; 12:7; and Mark 12:33). Journal this week about how you have experienced God's mercy because you called on him and saw him deliver you. In Psalm 50, the Israelites haven't called out for help, yet God has mercy and gives them this word to rescue them from ritual, which won't give them life. Instead, God brings them to a real relationship with him, which will give them life. When has God delivered you without your asking for help?

4

Broken for You

What lengths are we willing to go to show Jesus how much we value him? The answer lies in whether we grasp how deeply Jesus values us.

GROUP DISCUSSION. Today's study has to do with what we value. Besides the Bible or your salvation, what is your most valuable possession? Don't try to sound super spiritual; think of something you own that, if sold, would be worth some cold, hard cash. If it also has immense personal value, all the better.

PERSONAL REFLECTION. Do you struggle to believe that Jesus really cares about you? Spend some time telling Jesus about this; ask him to help you see how much he values you.

In this passage Jesus has journeyed to Jerusalem for the last time and is eating at a friend's home outside of Jerusalem. An anonymous woman, identified as Mary Magdalene in John's Gospel, breaks a vessel of perfume worth a large amount of money and pours it over Jesus' head. *Read Mark 14:1-11.*

1. Imagine yourself in this scene: what do you see, hear, smell, feel, think?

What might be a parallel situation today?

2. Tensions ran high. What are the various conflicts in this passage, and who is involved?

3. Jesus has shown previously he cares for the poor (Mark 10:21). What does he say about the poor here?

What does he say about himself?

4. Some of the guests call what the woman does a "waste." In contrast, Jesus calls it a "beautiful thing." What does the woman seem to understand that the others do not?

5. When have you been told that you were wasting something precious that you gave up to honor Jesus, or when have you thought that about another person?

6. Why do you think Jesus emphasizes that this story will be told "wherever the gospel is preached throughout the world . . . in memory of her" (v. 9)?

7. Contrast Judas's response to Jesus with the woman's (vv. 10-11).

Given what has just taken place, what might have provoked Judas to abandon Jesus and switch sides?

8. In the next section of Mark, Jesus eats the Passover with his disciples. Similar to the woman's actions of breaking the jar and pouring out the costly perfume to show how much she values Jesus, Jesus will break and pour out himself (Mark 14:22, 24), showing how much he values people by giving his life for them. Consider how often you think about how much Jesus loves you. How might a greater awareness of Jesus' love for you change the way you worship, or even your life?

9. Make a list of things you value highly (such as possessions, skills, activities and relationships).

Which of these might be more valuable to you than your relationship with Jesus?

What would it look like for you to use one or more of these things to worship Jesus?

Spend time thanking Jesus that he voluntarily died because he valued you greater than his own life.

Now or Later

Worship, as this woman exhibits, involves expressing our love and devotion to Jesus, at times in ways that others won't understand. Is there any way you have been holding back from God, in worship or in your daily life, possibly because you're afraid of the response of others? Try telling God about this, and then take action in spite of your fears.

Reflect on how this passage might deepen the significance of your practice of Communion.

5

Plantings of Praise

Our praise and worship are not meant to be limited to us, contained within the walls of our worshiping space. Instead God wants our praise to affect others and spread—throughout our neighborhoods and even the world. God compares his worshipers to a strong and beautiful stand of trees that show off his nutrient-rich soil, his expert gardening skills and his status as a master arborist. God has a plan for causing praise to multiply and we are an integral part.

GROUP DISCUSSION. Tell about the last time you were given the royal treatment. (Was it at the hands of a friend, in a hotel or restaurant, or at a significant life event? How did you feel afterward? Did anyone notice a difference in you, or did you tell anyone about it?)

PERSONAL REFLECTION. Which more accurately describes how you see yourself today: an "[oak] of righteousness, a planting of the LORD for the display of his splendor" (Isaiah 61:3) or "an oak with fading leaves, like a garden without water" (Isaiah 1:30)?

Why do you think you feel the way you do?

The book of Isaiah paints the full scope of God's judgment and redemption in vivid color and detail. In the second half of the book are four prophecies (sometimes called "servant songs") that unveil and celebrate the Messiah (Hebrew for "anointed one") and describe his mission. God had crowned Israel "a kingdom of priests" (Exodus 19:6), but they would always fall short; they would never be able to atone for the sins of the world. Enter Christ (Greek for "anointed one")—he is the perfected "Israel" in whom God will display his splendor (Isaiah 49:3) and through whom a righteous world order will result in God being globally praised. *Read Isaiah 61:1-11.*

---

1. There are two distinct voices in this passage—the anointed servant (or the prophet) and the Lord who sends the servant. How would you summarize in a sentence the heart of what each one says? (Try saying it as if you were the person speaking.)

---

2. The first speaker says he has something for various groups of suffering people: the poor, the brokenhearted, the captives, the prisoners (or the blind), the mourners and those who despair. In what way do you identify with one of these groups?

---

3. What seems to be the Lord's purpose in commissioning this servant?

---

4. What promises does the Lord's servant (and then the Lord) make to those whom he lifts up, heals, sets free and comforts?

What words and images from these promises particularly stand out to you?

---

5. How does what the servant brings these suffering people transform them into "oaks of righteousness," and what does this title imply (v. 3)?

---

6. When have you seen someone Jesus healed, provided for or set free become a "display of his splendor" to others?

---

7. How does the Lord want his people to be seen by the rest of the world (vv. 8-9)?

How do you reconcile the reality that Christians experience sadness, struggle and tragedy with the statement that all who see God's people will say they are blessed?

---

8. Why is being "arrayed in a robe of righteousness" cause for such jubilant praise (v. 10)?

9. From what you see in this passage, what do you think is the relationship between righteousness and praise?

10. What clothes from your old life—clothes that have nothing to do with salvation or righteousness—are you trying to hold onto?

How might you envision these clothes in a way that will encourage you to get rid of them?

11. What does your worshiping community (church, fellowship or study group) need from God to become a stronger, healthier planting that displays his righteousness and splendor?

Ask God to rid you of your old clothes and increase your comfort wearing his garments of salvation and praise. Pray also about your response to the final question.

Now or Later

Find a contemporary example of each of the suffering groups mentioned in Isaiah 61:1-3. The example may be one person or a collective group, someone you know personally or only know of, people in your city or people in another region or country. How might you or your study group bring to these people good news, bandages and healing, freedom, the Lord's favor, comfort, provision, or beauty, gladness and praise? If you only have time or resources for one person or group, choose one, find a way to reach them this week, and watch righteousness and praise spring up!

6

All to Jesus

**Luke 20:20-26,
45-47; 21:1-4**

We want to draw closer to Jesus, but we don't know how. Often, we vacillate between anxious striving and hopeless inaction, and of course neither helps us to know his acceptance or to worship him more fully. What if the answer was as simple as honesty? Though the Lord knows everything in our hearts whether we show him or not, our showing him is a sign of trust and deepens our relationship with him as well as our worship.

GROUP DISCUSSION. Have you ever been dishonest or deceitful, for example to get something that you wanted or to make yourself look good? What was the outcome, and how did you feel afterward?

PERSONAL REFLECTION. How easy is it for you to be honest with God? Do you talk to Jesus as often and as openly as you would a good friend? If there's anything you've been avoiding talking to him about, try talking with him about it now.

Nothing escapes the notice of Jesus. He sees all—our attempts to evade or trick him and our attempts to honor and trust him. *Read Luke 20:20-26.*

1. The chief priests, teachers of the law and elders had challenged Jesus' authority to throw out moneychangers and to teach in the temple. Jesus never let them get the upper hand. How are they now trying to trap him?

What do you think about their attempts?

_____

2. What does Jesus immediately know about the spies, and how does he avoid their trap?

_____

3. If we are stamped with the likeness of God, what does it mean for us to give to God what is his?

What areas of your life are you withholding, or most tempted to withhold, from God?

_____

4. *Read Luke 20:45-47.* From Jesus' description of the teachers of the law, what would you say they value most?

How does their attitude manifest itself in worship?

5. *Read Luke 21:1-4.* How do you respond to what Jesus says about those giving their offerings?

6. How does Jesus' awareness of the widow and her situation encourage you about a situation you now face (or how might you encourage someone else with Jesus' words)?

7. What common themes and contrasts run through Jesus' interaction with the spies, his warning about the teachers of the law and his affirmation of the poor widow?

8. From this passage, what do you think God wants from his worshipers?

What do you think God wants from *you*?

9. What is one thing you could do or give this week that would require you to increase your trust level beyond where it currently is?

Ask God to help you have no pretense with him and to make you more like the poor widow. Pray as simply and honestly as you know how.

Now or Later

Read 2 Corinthians 8:1-15. Giving money to provide for others' needs is a crucial part of Christian worship. Spend time thinking about how you make decisions regarding financial giving. How do the Macedonians' example and Paul's teaching in this passage encourage you to reconsider your views and current practice of giving? Share any new commitments you make with a trusted Christian friend who can encourage you to follow through.

7

Living Worship

Romans 12:1-8

So God wants *all* of you. Jesus instructed: "Give to God what is God's." God is reaching out to you every day, encouraging you to entrust yourself to him. What causes you to hold back? Some of us fear that giving our whole selves to God will mean giving up what we love to do, the passions and pursuits that we enjoy. In fact, sacrificing ourselves to God means becoming who we were intended to be.

GROUP DISCUSSION. Talk about something to which you've dedicated your life.

PERSONAL REFLECTION. Consider your body. How do you feel about it, treat it, use it (or abuse it)? What does your body enable you to do day in and day out?

Paul had some radical ideas about worship for his day, and for ours. He has spent the first eleven chapters of Romans discussing theology, emphasizing God's mercy and grace. Now he turns to application. *Read Romans 12:1-8.*

1. What commands does Paul give the Roman church, and what promises (implicit or explicit) does he offer?

---

2. How do you respond to the idea of being a living sacrifice?

---

3. The word "worship" in verse one comes from a Greek word *latreia* that originally meant "work done for hire or pay" and then "service" and eventually "that to which a person gives his or her whole life." What words and images does Paul use to describe worship, and what do they connote?

---

4. What is the connection between the worship Paul describes and God's will?

---

5. How have you been transformed in terms of your character, nature or mindset since becoming a Christian (v. 2)?

---

6. What is the outcome of presenting our bodies as living sacrifices, of being transformed by the renewing of our minds—particularly in terms of how we view ourselves and others?

7. What about the human body makes it a fitting metaphor for those of us who are "in Christ" (v. 5)?

How does Paul want Christians to relate?

8. What connections do you see in this passage between belief (what one thinks) and action (what one does)?

9. In verses 6-8, Paul mentions a number of gifts—not an exhaustive list—and tells people to use whatever gift has been given to them. Why might they have not been using their gifts?

Do you have a gift from God that you're not using? Why?

10. How would you define worship after studying this passage?

11. Consider your daily work and activities. How could you do them as worship to God?

Thank God for giving you gifts, skills and passions with which you can worship him every day. Remembering God's mercy (12:1), offer your whole self as a worship offering to him.

Now or Later

God is three in one—Father, Son and Holy Spirit. In his very being God models the unified community he designed his people to be (Romans 12:5). Worship is the gift of participating in the love of the Father and Son through the Holy Spirit who lives within us. Read and reflect on John 16:7-15; Romans 8:5-16; 2 Corinthians 1:22; and 1 John 4:13 to learn more about the crucial role of the Holy Spirit in Christian worship. What do these Scriptures say or imply about how the Holy Spirit makes worship possible, particularly the life-giving, life-encompassing worship Paul describes in Romans 12?

8

Our Longing Fulfilled

Revelation 21:1-8

A new world awaits us—a world where all our longings are fulfilled in God. The book of Revelation describes a future time when God will rule over a renovated universe. Without a belief in this future our worship and our lives lack significance and hope. We may even lose interest in worship, a deathblow to our relationship with God.

GROUP DISCUSSION. What is something you're looking forward to? How does what you're anticipating affect your actions and mood in the present?

PERSONAL REFLECTION. What do you fear the most? Spend some time imagining life without that fear or the looming threat of death, without pain or mourning or the fear of catastrophe. Imagine a place where you can talk with Jesus face-to-face and he walks among the people who love him. Ask God to help you believe that this life and place are coming realities.

"The revelation of Jesus Christ" (Revelation 1:1) was given by God to Jesus, who made it known to John, one of his apostles, through an angel. The Roman authorities, increasingly threatened by the spread of the gospel, had imprisoned John on the island of Patmos for his activities as a Christian missionary. *Read Revelation 21:1-8.*

1. What promises about the future does John receive through what he sees and hears?

Which of these promises do you look forward to the most, and why?

2. Looking at the whole passage, what will pass away and what will not pass away?

3. What does the metaphor of "a bride beautifully dressed for her husband" (v. 2) tell us about God's intentions and desires for his people? (See also Revelation 19:6-8.)

4. In verse three, John hears a loud voice from "the throne" (Revelation 20:11). Read Revelation 4, where the one sitting on the throne is described. What stands out to you about the promise that God will live with people (21:3)?

5. It had been said in other places that God would dwell among people. When this occurs finally and fully, how will it change life as we know it?

6. How does the promise that "there will be no more death or mourning or crying or pain" (v. 4) encourage you in a situation you're facing right now?

7. What does God mean when he says, "I am the Alpha and the Omega, the Beginning and the End" (v. 6)?

8. What characterizes those whose place "will be in the fiery lake of burning sulfur" (v. 8)?

9. How easy or difficult is it for you to believe that this picture is an actual representation of your personal future?

How might you keep the reality of God's eventual reign and abolishment of death and suffering more central in your life?

10. "When the end of history is fully understood, its impact radically affects the present."* How does this passage encourage you to persist in worshiping God now and for the rest of your life?

Thank God for what you have to look forward to and for how he allows you to experience tastes of heaven now through worship.

Now or Later

Reflect on these passages that affirm God's promise-keeping nature: Joshua 23:14; Psalm 33:9-11; Isaiah 46:10-11; Mark 13:31; Romans 4:20-21; 2 Peter 3:8-14. His words always come true, which means that what he has said in Revelation will materialize.

Take one worship scene from Revelation a day, and use the hymns of praise as the basis for your own praise of God: 4:1-11; 5:6-14; 7:9-17; 11:15-19; 15:1-8; 19:1-10.

---

*Bruce Wilkinson and Kenneth Boa, *Talk Through the Bible* (Nashville: Thomas Nelson, 1983), p. 513.

Leader's Notes

MY GRACE IS SUFFICIENT FOR YOU. (2 COR 12:9)

Leading a Bible discussion can be an enjoyable and rewarding experience. But it can also be *scary*—especially if you've never done it before. If this is your feeling, you're in good company. When God asked Moses to lead the Israelites out of Egypt, he replied, "O LORD, please send someone else to do it" (Ex 4:13). It was the same with Solomon, Jeremiah and Timothy, but God helped these people in spite of their weaknesses, and he will help you as well.

You don't need to be an expert on the Bible or a trained teacher to lead a Bible discussion. The idea behind these inductive studies is that the leader guides group members to discover for themselves what the Bible has to say. This method of learning will allow group members to remember much more of what is said than a lecture would.

These studies are designed to be led easily. As a matter of fact, the flow of questions through the passage from observation to interpretation to application is so natural that you may feel that the studies lead themselves. This study guide is also flexible. You can use it with a variety of groups—student, professional, neighborhood or church groups. Each study takes forty-five to sixty minutes in a group setting.

There are some important facts to know about group dynamics and encouraging discussion. The suggestions listed below should enable you to effectively and enjoyably fulfill your role as leader.

Preparing for the Study

1. Ask God to help you understand and apply the passage in your own life. Unless this happens, you will not be prepared to lead others. Pray too for the various members of the group. Ask God to open your hearts to the message of his Word and motivate you to action.

2. Read the introduction to the entire guide to get an overview of the entire book and the issues which will be explored.

3. As you begin each study, read and reread the assigned Bible passage to familiarize yourself with it.

4. This study guide is based on the New International Version of the Bible. It will help you and the group if you use this translation as the basis for your study and discussion.

5. Carefully work through each question in the study. Spend time in meditation and reflection as you consider how to respond.

6. Write your thoughts and responses in the space provided in the study guide. This will help you to express your understanding of the passage clearly.

7. It might help to have a Bible dictionary handy. Use it to look up any unfamiliar words, names or places. (For additional help on how to study a passage, see chapter five of *How to Lead a LifeBuilder Study,* IVP, 2018.)

8. Consider how you can apply the Scripture to your life. Remember that the group will follow your lead in responding to the studies. They will not go any deeper than you do.

9. Once you have finished your own study of the passage, familiarize yourself with the leader's notes for the study you are leading. These are designed to help you in several ways. First, they tell you the purpose the study guide author had in mind when writing the study. Take time to think through how the study questions work together to accomplish that purpose. Second, the notes provide you with additional background information or suggestions on group dynamics for various questions. This information can be useful when people have difficulty understanding or answering a question. Third, the leader's notes can alert you to potential problems you may encounter during the study.

10. If you wish to remind yourself of anything mentioned in the leader's notes, make a note to yourself below that question in the study.

Leading the Study

1. Begin the study on time. Open with prayer, asking God to help the group to understand and apply the passage.

2. Be sure that everyone in your group has a study guide. Encourage the group to prepare beforehand for each discussion by reading the introduction to the guide and by working through the questions in the study.

3. At the beginning of your first time together, explain that these studies are meant to be discussions, not lectures. Encourage the members of the group to participate. However, do not put pressure on those who may be hesitant to speak during the first few sessions. You may want to suggest the following guidelines to your group.

☐ Stick to the topic being discussed.

☐ Your responses should be based on the verses which are the focus of the discussion and not on outside authorities such as commentaries or speakers.

☐ These studies focus on a particular passage of Scripture. Only rarely should you refer to other portions of the Bible. This allows for everyone to participate in in-depth study on equal ground.

☐ Anything said in the group is considered confidential and will not be discussed outside the group unless specific permission is given to do so.

☐ We will listen attentively to each other and provide time for each person present to talk.

☐ We will pray for each other.

4. Have a group member read the introduction at the beginning of the discussion.

5. Every session begins with a group discussion question. The question or activity is meant to be used before the passage is read. The question introduces the theme of the study and encourages group members to begin to open up. Encourage as many members as possible to participate, and be ready to get the discussion going with your own response.

This section is designed to reveal where our thoughts or feelings need to be transformed by Scripture. That is why it is especially important not to read the passage before the discussion question is asked. The passage will tend to color the honest reactions people would otherwise give because they are, of course, supposed to think the way the Bible does.

You may want to supplement the group discussion question with an ice-breaker to help people to get comfortable. See the community section of the *Small Group Starter Kit* (IVP, 1995) for more ideas.

You also might want to use the personal reflection question with your group. Either allow a time of silence for people to respond individually or discuss it together.

6. Have a group member (or members if the passage is long) read aloud the passage to be studied. Then give people several minutes to read the passage again silently so that they can take it all in.

7. Question 1 will generally be an overview question designed to briefly survey the passage. Encourage the group to look at the whole passage, but try to avoid getting sidetracked by questions or issues that will be addressed later in the study.

8. As you ask the questions, keep in mind that they are designed to be used just as they are written. You may simply read them aloud. Or you may prefer to express them in your own words.

There may be times when it is appropriate to deviate from the study guide.

For example, a question may have already been answered. If so, move on to the next question. Or someone may raise an important question not covered in the guide. Take time to discuss it, but try to keep the group from going off on tangents.

9. Avoid answering your own questions. If necessary, repeat or rephrase them until they are clearly understood. Or point out something you read in the leader's notes to clarify the context or meaning. An eager group quickly becomes passive and silent if they think the leader will do most of the talking.

10. Don't be afraid of silence. People may need time to think about the question before formulating their answers.

11. Don't be content with just one answer. Ask, "What do the rest of you think?" or "Anything else?" until several people have given answers to the question.

12. Acknowledge all contributions. Try to be affirming whenever possible. Never reject an answer. If it is clearly off-base, ask, "Which verse led you to that conclusion?" or again, "What do the rest of you think?"

13. Don't expect every answer to be addressed to you, even though this will probably happen at first. As group members become more at ease, they will begin to truly interact with each other. This is one sign of healthy discussion.

14. Don't be afraid of controversy. It can be very stimulating. If you don't resolve an issue completely, don't be frustrated. Move on and keep it in mind for later. A subsequent study may solve the problem.

15. Periodically summarize what the group has said about the passage. This helps to draw together the various ideas mentioned and gives continuity to the study. But don't preach.

16. At the end of the Bible discussion you may want to allow group members a time of quiet to work on an idea under "Now or Later." Then discuss what you experienced. Or you may want to encourage group members to work on these ideas between meetings. Give an opportunity during the session for people to talk about what they are learning.

17. Conclude your time together with conversational prayer, adapting the prayer suggestion at the end of the study to your group. Ask for God's help in following through on the commitments you've made.

18. End on time.

Many more suggestions and helps are found in *How to Lead a LifeBuilder Study*.

Components of Small Groups

A healthy small group should do more than study the Bible. There are four components to consider as you structure your time together.

Nurture. Small groups help us to grow in our knowledge and love of God. Bible study is the key to making this happen and is the foundation of your small group.

Community. Small groups are a great place to develop deep friendships with other Christians. Allow time for informal interaction before and after each study. Plan activities and games that will help you get to know each other. Spend time having fun together—going on a picnic or cooking dinner together.

Worship and prayer. Your study will be enhanced by spending time praising God together in prayer or song. Pray for each other's needs—and keep track of how God is answering prayer in your group. Ask God to help you to apply what you are learning in your study.

Outreach. Reaching out to others can be a practical way of applying what you are learning, and it will keep your group from becoming self-focused. Host a series of evangelistic discussions for your friends or neighbors. Clean up the yard of an elderly friend. Serve at a soup kitchen together, or spend a day working in the community.

Many more suggestions and helps in each of these areas are found in the *Small Group Starter Kit.* You will also find information on building a small group. Reading through the starter kit will be worth your time.

Study 1. Soul Satisfaction.
Psalm 63.

Purpose: To root our worship in God's character, particularly his great love and faithfulness.

Group discussion. This question about advertising can be a light and fun way to start off the study, but it may also stir some individuals' consciences as they consider where they've been looking for satisfaction.

If you want to deepen the opening discussion or if you prefer an alternate way to begin, you might say, "Mick Jagger exclaimed, 'I can't get no . . . satisfaction!' People worldwide relate to this sentiment, thus the popularity of the song. Have you ever felt completely satisfied? If so, what was the situation, and what enabled you to feel this way? If not, what keeps you from being so?"

Question 1. In preparing for this study, you may want to read 2 Samuel 15—17. Put yourself in David's position. How devastating would it be to have your own son (or a good friend) betray you in such a manner? Interestingly, 2 Samuel 15:23 foreshadows Jesus' walk through the Kidron Valley (Jn 18:1) after his friend and "sons" (Judas and the Jewish leaders) betray him.

The Kidron Valley is east of Jerusalem and dry most of the year. David is literally in the desert when he writes this psalm. Perhaps his physical condition and surroundings remind him of his spiritual need; they certainly serve as apt metaphors. He needs God in the same way that he needs water and food—it's a matter of survival. "Where there is no water" (Ps 63:1): Jerusalem had no river, unlike surrounding cities. However, it had a river in the form of God's sustaining, refreshing and perpetual presence (see Ps 36:8 and 46:4).

Psalms served as the temple hymnal and devotional guide of the Jewish people; many were sung (the word *psalm* comes from a Greek word meaning "a song sung to the accompaniment of a plucked instrument"), and early church leaders prescribed Psalm 63 for daily public prayers. The spirit, attitude and message David conveys are fundamental to worship.

David follows the most common literary format for a psalm: an initial expression of longing or desperation turns into a confident and joyful declaration of God's expected provision. God will set all things right.

Question 2. Being spiritually hungry and thirsty is a positive thing, although the circumstances surrounding our deprivation may be extremely difficult (as was the case for King David). This question, therefore, has the potential to take the study down a very personal path, and people may need encouragement to open up. Be prepared to give a response of your own if no one leads out; in this way you can model the truth that even Bible study leaders experience dry and desperate times.

Question 3. David has encountered God's profound love (v. 3) and his help and protection (v. 7). *Love* in Hebrew is a rich and complex word that connotes lovingkindness, favor, goodness and mercy all at once; it is the chief character trait of God.

Note the difference between Psalm 62:11-12 where David says he has *heard* that God is strong and loving and Psalm 63:2 where he has seen for himself. The same distinction between hearing from others and seeing for oneself is made in Psalm 48:8. The word *glory* in Hebrew literally means "weight," figurative for splendor or copiousness (very plentiful, abundant wealth).

Question 4. God's unchanging nature, and not David's circumstances, inspire David's worship. Even as he worships, David is reminding himself that God is his protector: "shadow of your wings" (v. 7) is a conventional Hebrew metaphor that describes the protective expanse of God's power and his protection against oppression (as shade protects from the oppressive desert sun).

Question 5. Help people to grapple with the phrase "your love is better than life" (v. 3). Would they describe God's love in this way—why or why not? Have they encountered this love? Confidence in God's deep love for us is fundamental to worship and to our faith; at the same time, you can assure people that we often come to understand God's love over time as our relationship with him grows.

Question 6. Consider experiences from David's life in which he needed and experienced God's help and love firsthand: working as a shepherd, battling Goliath, being chosen king of Israel, running from King Saul, and needing God's forgiveness for his sins against Bathsheba and Uriah.

Hebrews divided the night into three watches: sunset to 10 p.m., 10 p.m. to 2 a.m., and 2 a.m. to sunrise. Throughout the night, David thinks about God. His remembrances enable him to declare confidently that God is his help (v. 7), to worship God instead of to despair.

Question 7. The relationship between God and humans is two-way, but the roles are completely different. David knows that he can only depend (he thirsts, longs, clings) and respond (with praise, lifting up hands and rejoicing). God sustains, protects, delivers, satisfies. Even though David's enemies seek his life, David seeks God, and in the end the fate his enemies have planned for him will become their own. Note that David contrasts "the mouths of liars" with "all who swear by God's name" (v. 11). In the end, those who trust and praise God will be vindicated.

Question 8. In the Hebrew mindset, the soul is not the spiritual dimension of a person in distinction from the physical. The soul is considered to be one's whole self as a living, conscious, personal being. Thus in verse one, when David says "my soul . . . my body," he is using two ways to say "my whole being."

Question 10. Encourage people to be as honest as possible regarding how they've been dissatisfied and to be as concrete as possible about an action they can take to pursue satisfaction in God. To promote honesty and concreteness, have the group write down their thoughts. Revealing their answers can be optional.

Now or Later. You may want to encourage people to have a journal to record their thoughts and prayers as they proceed through this Bible study. As we've seen in Psalm 63, the ability to remember what God has done or revealed of himself is foundational to worship; having a written record (like the psalms and all of Scripture) helps us not to forget.

Study 2. For Keeps. Exodus 24:1-11.

Purpose: To see that in worship we recall and celebrate again and again the covenant God has made with us whereby he has promised to be our keeper and we have promised to be kept.

Group discussion. Apt examples could be a marriage, other family relationships or close friendships. In my marriage, for example, we eat dinner together every night that we can, talk to each other at least once during the workday, practice a weekly date night and annually write our year's memories in a special commemorative book. These traditions are meaningful because they signify our commitment to one another and deepen our love, as worship traditions are meant to do for believers and God.

Question 1. Before the covenant is sealed: verses 1-5. The covenant being sealed: verses 6-8. Celebrating the covenant: verses 9-11.

A covenant is a binding agreement or pact made by two parties. Covenants, or treaties, were common in Near Eastern practice between kings, or between kings and their vassals, so covenant language would have been familiar to the Israelites. God had made covenants with Noah (Gen 9) and Abraham (Gen 15; 17) before Exodus 24. His covenant with Abraham is referenced in Exodus 2 and 6 when Scripture says God remembered his covenant with Abraham, Isaac and Jacob, which was to give them the land of Canaan. The nearest reference to a covenant before Exodus 24 is in Exodus 19:5. Here God makes it clear that his intention is not only to give the Israelites land but to make them his "treasured possession . . . a kingdom of priests and a holy nation." At the core of the "Sinaitic covenant" (because it was ratified on Mt. Sinai), then, is God's desire for Israel to have a unique relationship with him that reveals to the whole world God's sovereignty, righteousness, mercy and love.

A covenant establishes a committed relationship, similar to marriage vows. The covenant-maker is concerned for the good and protection of the other, not simply himself (versus our view of contracts today). See Jeremiah 3:14 and 31:32—which refers directly to the covenant of Exodus 24—where God calls himself Israel's husband.

Question 2. Examples might include marriages, renewals of wedding vows, baptisms or baby dedications, adoption legalizations, bar/bat mitzvahs, naturalization ceremonies, or current-day worship services—any events where vows are made or remembered and relationships are established or forged.

Question 3. The people respond with one voice, meaning they are in wholehearted and unified agreement that they will obey *everything* the Lord has said. In other words, they agree to the terms of the covenant as laid out in Exodus 20:2—23:33. The people had agreed to obey earlier as well, when Moses first mentioned the covenant (Ex 19:8). After the people respond in Exodus 24:3, Moses writes down the Lord's words, making the terms of the covenant more permanent. Only after the people hear Moses read the written words and affirm again that they will obey God does Moses "seal the deal" with blood. The multistage process gives the sense that this is a serious and binding commitment.

Question 4. The "Book of the Covenant" refers to God's ordinances for his people found in Exodus 20—23 (what Moses had just written down). To fulfill their role as a "kingdom of priests and a holy nation" (Ex 19:5), God's people need to know and obey God's words. The same is true today. If we are to experience the benefits of the covenant God has made with us, we must not only listen to but also understand the essence of and live out God's words. The Bible is our Book of the Covenant and should play a central role in Christian worship. In worship we need to hear God's Word and to experience the Living Word, Jesus; listening receptively to the Word of God is an act of worship as profound as singing any song.

If someone raises the point that because of Christ's death and resurrection, Christians live under the new covenant, and grace has triumphed over law, you may want to direct people to Jeremiah 31:31-33 where the new covenant is introduced, so that they can read it for themselves. The essence of this covenant is the same as all covenants before it: God will be our God and we will be God's people. To be God's people means to obey him as Lord. God's law (v. 33) will still maintain its significance as something for us to know and follow. The emphasis of the new covenant is not our obedience, however, but God's commitment to fulfill the promises of the covenant on both sides—in other words, his solution for the problem of our sinfulness through the sacrifice of Jesus. God is so devoted to us he wants to ensure the permanence of our relationship with him. Jesus fulfills our side of the covenant so that we can continue to be the people of God in spite of our failings, but he never said we no longer need to obey God. On the contrary, he called people to higher levels of obedience (see Mt 5:17). If the discussion becomes a debate about obedience and salvation, try to bring it back around to remembering and celebrating God's covenant as a central purpose of worship.

Question 5. Blood is sprinkled on the altar, symbolizing God's forgiveness and acceptance of the sacrifice, and on the people, signifying they have been bound to God with their oath of obedience. Robert Webber points out, "In the Old Testament God always used a blood sacrifice to demonstrate the sealing of a relationship with people" (*Worship Old and New* [Grand Rapids, Mich.: Zondervan, 1994], p. 21). This is the first time in the Bible that the phrase "the blood of the covenant" is used. Jesus uses a similar phrase in Mark 14:24, except that he says, "This is *my* blood of the covenant" (emphasis added). He will shed his blood to the point of death for the sake of humanity. Exodus 24:8 foreshadows the blood of the covenant that will bind to the Lord all those who put their faith in Jesus as their deliverer.

Question 7. Two parties who made a covenant often celebrated their alliance with a "covenantal meal" (see Gen 26:30; 31:54). Sharing a meal is an expression of fellowship. It is possible that this eating and drinking foreshadows the Lord's Supper that we celebrate in worship to remember Jesus' sacrifice, which permanently sealed God's covenant with us. What the leaders see when they enter God's presence is very similar to Ezekiel's experience of God in Ezekiel 1:26-28.

Question 8. God is saying he is serious about this relationship. He rescued his people from slavery for a purpose—to be in a relationship with them that would be a witness and light to all the nations, a relationship that would be "for keeps." This Old Testament ceremony is a model for what we do every time we gather to worship together, for while the Exodus was the greatest act of God's salvation in the Old Testament, we celebrate the greatest act of God's salvation ever in the gift of Jesus.

Question 10. Consider each element of a worship service and how it could help you remember God's covenant with you: the call to worship, music and singing, reading of the Word, the sermon, baptisms, Communion, prayer, the benediction, fellowship with other believers (and in some traditions, the passing of the peace).

Study 3. Mercy, Not Sacrifice. Psalm 50.

Purpose: To see that God does not rebuff the activities of our ritualized worship but that he more eagerly desires to have our trust, to communicate his presence and, most of all, to show us his mercy.

Group discussion. Answers could range from the lighthearted to serious difficulties. Be prepared for the latter, and if the opportunity arises, you could offer to pray briefly for the person right then or at the end of the study. The point is to help people feel comfortable talking in the group and to set a relational tone. The point is *not* to "test" people on whether they responded to their dilemmas with prayer or by calling out to God.

Personal reflection. God could show you anything as you reflect and listen to him about this. God showed me in worship that the "something that's of worth" was me . . . was all of us worshiping him at that moment. We are valuable and bless God's heart.

Question 1. In Deuteronomy, Moses renews the covenant with the people. He calls on heaven and earth to serve as third-party witnesses to the fact that the people have agreed to worship and obey God alone (Deut 30:19; 31:28;

32:1). In Psalm 50 the Lord again calls on heaven and earth to testify with him that his words are just and in accordance with the covenant.

This question is meant to provide an overview of the psalm; answers could come from anywhere in the passage. It is important to see that God is still committed to Israel. He calls them "my people" and reaffirms that he is their God (v. 7). He doesn't back out when they (or we) renege. What the people are *not* doing is implied in God's directives.

Question 2. God affirms that the covenant with him was made by sacrifice (v. 5). He doesn't have a problem with the act of sacrifice in and of itself (v. 8).

Question 3. To start off, the description of God in the first six verses paints a picture of a mighty force, not to be reckoned with. This God has the power to summon planets and stars; his presence electrifies the atmosphere. His power and holiness literally take the form of a raging fire that precedes him. This is the same God who met the Israelites on Mount Sinai after he expressed the intention of his covenant for them (Ex 19:16-19).

You might have people identify the various names and titles used for God in this psalm. "The Mighty One, God, the LORD" (v. 1) appears only one other time in Scripture, in Joshua 22:22. There, certain tribes of Israel denied any disobedience on their parts and announced that if they had been rebellious in their hearts, building their own altars to turn away from the Lord, they wanted the Lord himself to call them to account. In Psalm 50 this is exactly what God is doing—calling his people to account before they stray too far.

In verse 21, the Hebrew word for "I was" is the same word God uses for himself as a name when he tells Moses to say to the Israelites, "I AM has sent me to you" (Ex 3:14). This name, which literally means to exist or to be, expresses God's character as eternal, dependable and faithful, and therefore as deserving of his people's complete and perpetual trust.

Question 4. The sacrifices were meant to remind the Israelites of God's mercy and forgiveness, to stress that God desires a relationship with his people and therefore provides a means to deal with the real barrier of sin. It would appear that they were bringing sacrifices to appease God or to fulfill their religious duty, rather than out of a desire to honor or draw close to him. This quote from C. S. Lewis provides a helpful perspective: "It is in the process of being worshipped that God communicates His presence to men. . . . Even in Judaism the essence of the sacrifice was not really that men gave bulls and goats to God, but that by their so doing God gave Himself to men" (*Reflections on the Psalms*).

Question 5. God's commands in verses 14 and 15 point to a God who desires us to give him *ourselves* (not primarily objects apart from ourselves) in the form of warm and grateful hearts, willing and obedient spirits, and dependent and trusting requests for help. Trusting God—demonstrated through gratitude, obedience and dependence—honors God and enables us to encounter him most powerfully. *The point of worship is to build and deepen our trust of God as we receive his mercy.*

Question 6. To be clear, the commands are "sacrifice thank offerings" (v. 14, be grateful and express your gratefulness), "fulfill your vows" (v. 14, do what you say you will, be obedient to what God tells you to do), and "call upon me in the day of trouble" (v. 15, pray, ask God for help, continually recognize your dependence on God). "I will deliver you, and you will honor me" (v. 15) are natural outcomes of trusting God. God can be counted on to make good on his word.

Question 7. Help people to search themselves as to whether they are guilty of any of these violations, even marginally. Awareness and conviction always precede confession and repentance. Have they ignored God's instruction (v. 17)? Have they taken what wasn't theirs or committed adultery in their hearts (v. 18)? Do they engage in gossip or lying (v. 19)? Do they speak ill of others, even their own family members (v. 20)? If so, they don't need to beat themselves up, but they do need to ask God for forgiveness. He is faithful and just and has promised to forgive when asked (1 Jn 1:8-10). He is merciful.

When we fall into the trap of thinking that God is "soft on sin," like the world around us, or that his silence means he is condoning sin rather than expressing mercy and patience—when we convince ourselves that our actions won't have consequences—we wind up far from God.

Question 8. Gratitude makes us more receptive to what God has for us. Salvation is ultimately about receiving God (Jn 1:12). Speaking or showing our gratitude may help someone else see God's goodness and desire his salvation as well.

Question 9. Our attitude toward God (and sometimes toward others whom we project onto God) determines how we perceive God's words and actions—as merciful or demanding, loving or harsh. Some Israelites probably responded well to the message of Psalm 50; others probably did not. The same will be true today. God is always justified in his judgments, but his continual desire is for people to return to him and enjoy the benefits of being close to him. His desire is to show mercy (Is 1:10-20; Hos 2:14-20; Lk 13:34; Rom 2:4; 2 Pet 3:9).

Question 10. For example, it is easier for me to sing songs about God's forgiveness than to consider how I need God to forgive me, asking him to do so and truly receiving his mercy. It's easy to write a check and put it in the offering plate without taking time to thank God that he's provided me with money to give. It is easy to show up for church on Sunday but much harder to tell my husband I'm sorry when I do something inconsiderate afterward.

Prayer. If you are in a group, you could each write down one thing you are thankful for on a slip of paper with your name. Put the slips in a bowl and have each person choose one. Thank God out loud on behalf of one another for the things he is doing in your lives.

Study 4. Broken for You. Mark 14:1-11.

Purpose: To allow the extravagant gift God gave us in Jesus to increase our level of devotion to him.

Question 1. A denarius was equivalent to a day's wage. Three hundred denarii (or a year's wages) at today's minimum wage (approximately seven dollars an hour) would be $16,800. Nard is a perfume made from the aromatic oil extracted from the root of a plant grown mainly in India, making it a rare and precious treasure. The fact that her perfume was worth so much would indicate that it was probably an heirloom, perhaps even a part of her dowry. In breaking it open and pouring it out, she is divesting herself of a major source of family wealth and security, as well as her personal future hope. She is saying that Jesus is worth more.

Possible contemporary examples: someone spending all of their savings to give thousand-dollar tips to each of the wait staff at a party; someone pouring a fifteen-thousand-dollar bottle of champagne over the head of a winning coach.

Question 2. The larger context of this passage is that Jesus has recently been in Jerusalem where the crowds hailed him and he overturned moneychangers' tables in the temple and debated with the religious leaders. Bethany is about two miles from Jerusalem and apparently where he stayed at night. The holy city would be flooded with religious pilgrims making their annual visit for Passover and the week-long Feast of Unleavened Bread. Passover represented the deliverance of the Jews from the plague that killed the firstborn in Egyptian homes because their doors were not marked with the blood of a spotless lamb (Ex 11:1—12:30). It also foreshadowed Jesus' sacrifice.

This story is told in three Gospels. Matthew identifies the objectors to the woman's action as the disciples; John singles out Judas Iscariot as the prime objector. Mark's emphasis is not on who complains but on the action itself and the contrast between the woman's devotion and the hostility of the religious leaders and Judas.

Question 3. It was customary to give gifts to the poor on the evening of Passover (see Jn 13:29). Those who rebuke the woman for her prodigality may be expecting Jesus to praise them for their righteousness. If it is the disciples, they remain clueless about the trials that await Jesus, in spite of the many times he has tried to explain what he must go through.

Jesus' words about the poor are reminiscent of Deuteronomy 15:11, in which God says, "There will always be poor people in the land. Therefore I command you to be openhanded toward your brothers and toward the poor." Jesus chides them that they can help the poor anytime they want, if they're so eager, but he will soon be gone.

Question 4. Anointing was a common custom at feasts (Ps 23:5; Lk 7:46); this woman's lavishness, however, goes far beyond the norm. Most likely she is focusing on expressing her love and has no idea of the greater significance of her act, which points toward Jesus' suffering and death, as Jesus indicates. He says the woman has prepared his body for burial, underscoring that he is a suffering servant-king, not the conquering, culturally exclusive king the Jews are expecting.

What the woman did understand was Jesus' value. On the eve of his rejection, alienation and death she has shown him great affection, honor and love. The others' remarks are tantamount to saying that Jesus is not worth such an extravagant show of generosity, adding to his suffering.

Question 5. Remind people that Jesus calls any sacrifice made in love for him a "beautiful thing." It is never a waste.

Question 6. Jesus perhaps wants to encourage them that his death will not be final. Without the resurrection, there would be no gospel (or "good news") to preach. He is also letting them know that part of the plan is that his gospel will be preached throughout the world. Finally, he seems intent that this unnamed woman, whose action anticipated and prefigured his death, not be forgotten for her profound act of love.

Question 7. Mark does not explicitly tell us why Judas betrays Jesus. From the context, it is likely that Judas is starting to realize that Jesus is on his way out; he is not the Messiah Judas has hoped for. Judas rejects the opportunity to be on God's side, characterized by humility and making oneself the servant of all, and chooses the side of man, which tries to maintain control through wealth, power and prestige. He does not see the woman's act, or Jesus' pending sacrifice, as a beautiful thing, only a waste.

Question 8. The juxtaposition of the anointing and the Passover meal, and the parallel use of the words *broke* and *poured,* are undoubtedly intentional on Mark's part. He is drawing a connection for the reader so that we will understand Jesus' sacrifice as a sign of his love and devotion toward us, just as the woman's sacrifice was a sign of her love and devotion toward him. Jesus' extravagant gift—being broken for us—is what made the woman's act of worship so meaningful. In other words, the foundation of Christian worship is what God has done for us and not what we do for God. As we grasp how much he values us, we worship and live our lives with greater devotion.

Question 9. If you are leading a group, allow people time to make their lists and reflect on them.

Study 5. Plantings of Praise. Isaiah 61:1-11.

Purpose: To increase our desire for God's righteousness in our lives because righteousness causes us to praise God more.

Personal reflection. In Isaiah 1:30, the cause of the people's withering is their own sin and bad choices not to do right or worship God. As you reflect on your current spiritual and emotional state, consider your own role in your condition, as well as how others and life circumstances have contributed.

Question 1. Be sure to point out that there is no one right way to summarize the voice of the servant (vv. 1-7, 10-11) or the Lord (vv. 8-9). Different people will notice and emphasize different elements, potentially offering aspects others may have missed. Besides synthesizing the passage's content into a few summarizing statements, this question will enable people to get into the mindset of the servant of God (Christ and his followers) and God. Identifying in this way will help to reveal the speakers' priorities and the spirit behind their words.

Question 2. Look at what the "anointed one" offers to the group you identify with. Does this bring you any relief? You can be honest about this.

Question 3. The sovereign Lord desires people to be given their dignity and made whole. He wants them to have everlasting joy (v. 7). He also plans for them to serve as evidence of his redemptive work. Note that God receiving glory and people being well cared for are not mutually exclusive but actually interconnected. God sets up a win-win situation.

In the immediate context, Isaiah was predicting the return of Israel from the exile that occurred when they were captured and dispersed by Assyria and then Babylon. Cyrus from Persia conquered the Babylonians in 539 B.C. and the Jews returned home. This deliverance, the one proclaimed in Isaiah 61, foreshadowed God's greater rescue of people from our captivity to sin and death through Christ.

Question 4. Verses 3 and 10 provide powerful images of someone being dressed royally, receiving the royal treatment. Oil was used to anoint people during joyous occasions, as well as to treat wounds. Many other poignant images are used throughout the promises given.

Question 5. The word *righteousness* in Hebrew means rightness or justice and comes from a word that means to make right or be just. Those who are built up by the Lord will turn around and build up others (v. 4). They will minister to people and seek justice, even as they have been ministered to and received the fruits of justice. They will have all of their needs met and be filled with joy (vv. 6-7), which will show off God's righteousness. Most significantly, they will have an enduring relationship with the Lord (v. 8), who will enable them to remain righteous.

Question 7. The Hebrew word for *blessed* is applied to God in terms of an act of adoration, and to humans in terms of being benefited. In a sense, God does adore his people as well.

I once heard an African American pastor who grew up in the South during Jim Crow segregation say, "Sorrow can be the expositor of mysteries that joy can never explain." He went on to say that God didn't promise that we wouldn't have trials; he promised he would be with us through them (Is 43:2). This man was obviously blessed with wisdom forged from trusting God through difficult times. Scripture reminds us to "rejoice in our sufferings, because we know that suffering produces perseverance; perseverance, character; and character, hope" (Rom 5:3-4). Those with genuine hope attract the attention of a hopeless world. We will be called blessed not necessarily because our lives are struggle- and pain-free but because of how we respond to suffering—because we have a relationship with a God who cares.

Question 8. Consider where you would be if God had not chosen you as a recipient of his salvation and righteousness. At the center of Christian worship is what Jesus did for us, something we could never have done for ourselves. God has dressed us—"as a bridegroom . . . and as a bride." God's commitment to us is like that promised in a marriage. This is definitely cause for celebration.

Question 9. It is important to recognize that God is the rich soil from which any act of righteousness or praise will ever grow. He is also the one who tends the gardens of our hearts so that we want to be righteous like him and care about those who don't have good news, are brokenhearted or in bondage. As God cares for us and brings us into relationship with him, we praise him for who he is and what he has done for us (like the voice of verse 10). As his "oaks of righteousness," we then partner with him to administer to others what he has administered to us. In this way, justice, righteousness, mercy and peace continue to spread, and more praise will be the result.

Question 10. Some of us are wearing our old clothes on top of God's garments of salvation; others of us are hiding them in the form of underwear or tights. Maybe you don't wear the old clothes on your body but keep them stashed in the back of your closet in case you ever feel the urge to put them back on. See these old clothes for what they are: pants with too-tight waistlines, flagrant highwaters, an annoyingly scratchy sweater, a shirt with a huge stain. What do your old clothes look, feel and smell like? Ask God to take them to the trash!

Question 11. Consider how people in your church, fellowship and/or study group relate to one another as well as to those who need good news, the poor and brokenhearted, captives, prisoners, and the grieving. Righteousness gets lived out (or not) in these relationships, and don't forget: the source of all righteousness is always our relationship with God.

Study 6. All to Jesus. Luke 20:20-26, 45-47; 21:1-4.

Purpose: To see that in worship, what matters to Jesus is the amount of ourselves and of our trust given, our attitude toward others and our honesty toward God.

Group discussion. Dishonesty implies telling a lie or cheating. Deceit implies an intent to make someone believe what is not true, for example by putting on appearances. The point of these questions is to start getting in touch with how dishonesty and deceit build walls within ourselves, and between us and others, and us and God. Consider also the relationship between honesty and trust. Usually we are dishonest when we believe there's no other way to get what we need or want. We don't trust that God will provide for us. We may put on appearances because we don't trust that Jesus or others will accept us as we are.

For further discussion or as an alternative, ask people to discuss their response to the following quote from Rick Warren's *The Purpose-Driven Life*: "We can worship God imperfectly, but we cannot worship him insincerely" ([Grand Rapids, Mich.: Zondervan, 2002], p. 101).

Personal reflection. It's easy to be unaware of things we *aren't* talking to Jesus about. Most likely we're doing all we can to avoid thinking about whatever is bothering us, or we're spending a lot of time and energy thinking and worrying about it but not praying about it. Consider what perceptions of God hinder you from being completely honest with him or talking to him more regularly.

Question 1. The religious leaders wanted to provoke Jesus to say something against Rome. This would get him in trouble with the Roman governor and force him to leave off teaching the people, among whom he was gaining influence. Basically, they wanted the Roman officials to do their dirty work so that they wouldn't lose the favor of the people. The governor in this case was Pontius Pilate, governor of Judea. His official residence was some fifty miles away in Caesarea, but he stayed in Jerusalem during Passover to quell any trouble that might have arisen among the large crowds of Jews who came for the festival. It is ironic that the religious leaders denounced Jesus' authority (Lk 20:2) but recognized the governor's (20:20).

Question 2. You might also ask people what tone of voice they imagine the spies using as they talked to Jesus. Duplicity means "hypocritical cunning or deception; double-dealing." Jesus knew they were not genuine in their flattery; they just wanted to sound good. The spies expected Jesus to give them a straight yes-or-no answer. They most likely expected him to say no given their emphasis on him teaching "the way of God," which presumably would preclude giving Caesar any worship or tribute. If he said no, they would report him to Pilate. A yes response would make him unfavorable among the Jews, many of whom refused to pay taxes because they felt it was an admission of Rome's right to rule.

Jesus sidestepped the question of whether it's right to pay taxes and instead emphasized that they and all people, being imprinted with God's "portrait," belong to God and therefore need to give their lives over to him. God is the ultimate authority. By drawing a clear distinction between God and Caesar, he highlighted Caesar's idolatrous claim, stated in the coin's inscription: "Tiberius Caesar Augustus, son of the divine Augustus." He gave a passing nod to paying taxes while challenging anything less than full commitment to God, and they had nothing with which to accuse him.

Question 3. Consider every aspect of our beings—body, mind, soul, heart. Consider relationships, time, money, possessions, education, career, future, food, how you use your body and mind, and where your heart and soul are most invested. God wants to have input in every area of our lives because he made us and knows what will benefit us most. It's important that we make time to listen to the Holy Spirit in worship and prayer and respond with trust and obedience. As we give our whole selves to God's will, we will become more and more like Jesus.

Question 4. "The most important seats in the synagogues" refers to the bench in front of the enclosure that contained the Torah. Those who sat there could be seen by all who worshiped in the synagogue. Like the spies earlier, these religious leaders are concerned about sounding good (when they pray), not being genuine. They want to be noticed and esteemed. Jesus reveals that these leaders also deceive and exploit widows, a legally unprotected and vulnerable group at the time, presumably by taking their money when they should be helping to provide for them.

Question 5. Note in particular that Jesus starts off by saying, "I tell you the truth." Jesus, unlike the others we've seen in this passage, is honest. The widow's humble pennies are worth more than all of the wealthy people's gifts combined because she has given her all to God. She is in a position of needing to trust God one hundred percent, and she does—an act that doesn't escape Jesus' attention and praise. It's not the amount of money that matters but the amount of trust in God that she must have had to be able to give "all she had to live on" (v. 4).

Question 6. Jesus is fully aware of our attempts to trust him. He sees when we put ourselves out on a limb to follow him, and he will not let our faith go unrewarded (see Heb 11:6). He also honors what may look insignificant to the world, so when we're frustrated by our limitations (financial or otherwise) we can be encouraged that Jesus sees beyond amounts and into our hearts.

Question 7. This question is meant to be open-ended. Allow people to suggest multiple themes and contrasts. Hopefully, the discussion will crystallize the message of the passage and help tie the three scenes together, but you may need to summarize at the end. You could emphasize honesty versus duplicity, giving to God what is God's (as the widow does and as the religious leaders and Caesar do not), pretense in worship, the source of true authority, or how our level of surrender to God (that is, our humility) affects our attitude toward others and our worship.

Question 8. He wants the whole deal—every area of our lives and one hundred percent trust. He doesn't want pretense but genuineness. This means being honest in our prayers, confession, giving—in the whole way we present ourselves to him. To be honest requires humility, courage and faith.

Help people to consider how they personally put up "fronts" and how this affects their relationship with God and their worship. For many of us, there is a strong temptation not to be honest with God about our faults and shortcomings or questions and doubts. We labor under the illusion that we must clean ourselves up before coming to him, and our pride and fear keep us from receiving his grace, which would in turn deepen our worship.

Now or Later. Money, perhaps more than any idol in our culture, has the potential to sabotage our worship of God if we don't submit our attitudes and decisions about it to God. It is possible to worship money whether one has a lot or a little, because to worship money means to believe that it, and not God, is the key to "the good life." Jesus drew the distinction clearly: "You cannot serve both God and Money" (Mt 6:24).

Study 7. Living Worship. Romans 12:1-8.

Purpose: To accept Paul's (and God's) invitation to allow our whole lives to be worship so that we might know the heart and mind of God and be all we were meant to be.

Personal reflection. Your body is the temple of the Holy Spirit (1 Cor 6:19-20) and the instrument through which the Spirit works in the world. Whatever God wants to do through you, he will do through the body he's given you. The same was true for Jesus; he did not despise human flesh but took on his own. Spend time thanking God for your body (heart, mind, personality, limbs, organs—every part)!

Question 1. "Offer your bodies as living sacrifices": This command challenges the Greek mindset of the time that exalted the spirit and viewed the body as a prison to be despised and ashamed of. Paul is saying that for Christians, our bodies belong to God as much as our souls and we must worship him with our actions, as well as our minds. (See also Rom 6:11-13, 19.) It's not enough for us to offer things: possessions, money, material goods. We must offer our very selves. Note that we do this "in view of God's mercy." Jesus has been offered as the sacrifice that makes our relationship with God possible (Rom 3:22-25). "The heart overwhelmed with God's mercy is a worshiping heart" (Andy Park, *To Know You More* [Downers Grove, Ill.: InterVarsity Press, 2002], p. 52).

"Do not conform . . . but be transformed": We must avoid the temptation to model ourselves after the constantly changing outer world—with its disposition against the ways of God—and instead be changed from the inside out to be like Jesus. This command is a natural follow up to the one to offer our bodies: both mind and body must be surrendered to God.

Question 3. Worship is to be a whole-life affair. There's not a moment we're alive that can't be devoted to worshiping God. Even while we sleep, our continued breathing gives praise to our God who "will neither slumber nor sleep" but instead "watches over [us]" (Ps 121:3-4).

Regarding the phrase "living sacrifices": sacrifices accompanied worship rituals of the time; this would be a familiar image to his audience. As we've seen previously (Ex 24:8; Ps 50:5), sacrifices expressed a covenant commitment. Here we see that God wants *us* as sacrifices. Once an animal is sacrificed, it's dead; the sacrifice of ourselves to God, on the other hand, makes us more alive because we're coming to know (and presumably follow) God's good, pleasing and perfect will. We are "living sacrifices, holy and pleasing" because of the new life and righteousness God has given us through Jesus (for example, Rom 5:17-18).

Regarding the phrase "spiritual act of worship": "spiritual" implies that which is done with heart, mind and will, not merely a ritualistic exercise— the kind of worship offered by someone truly being him- or herself before God. The Greek for "spiritual worship" could also be translated as "reasonable worship" or "logical worship"—that is worship that makes sense from what we know. Once we taste God's mercy and get to know him even a little, it just makes sense that we would worship him.

Question 4. If we obey the commands of verses 1 and 2, we can know the will—the heart and mind—of God. His will is good (providing growth and blessing to those who trust him), pleasing (to those who know he is good) and perfect (no improvement can be made on it). True worship aligns our will with the Father's.

Question 5. Transformation is a process. Even if you're not night-and-day different, you can still answer this question. If you can't think of any way you've changed because of God's work in your life, consider why.

Question 6. Once we see ourselves as first and foremost dedicated to God's purposes, and every gift or talent we possess as from God to do his will, there is no longer any basis for competition or conceit. Our gifts are not primarily for gaining admiration (although that may come) but for serving others. We can gladly and humbly use our gifts, confident of the absolute value and necessity of our contribution. We come to see others not as threats or as useful means to our own selfish ends but as people to encourage to use their gifts the way God intended.

Question 7. The parts of a body don't argue, envy or dispute their relative importance; each part carries out its function so that the body can live and thrive. As Christians we are connected and interdependent; we need each other. We must act toward one another in a way that promotes health and furthers unity.

Question 8. If one person trusts another, especially in a relationship with a superior, that person will express his or her trust by doing what the other wishes. Our faith in God should naturally lead us to do what God wants (Ernest Best, *The Letter of Paul to the Romans* [Cambridge: Cambridge University Press, 1967], pp. 139-40).

If we believe God is merciful, we will offer our bodies as living sacrifices to him (v. 1). If we allow our minds to be renewed, our lives will look different from those following the pattern of the world (v. 2). If we think of ourselves rightly and understand the role God has for us to play, we will offer our gifts humbly, "in proportion to [our] faith" (vv. 3, 6).

To know God's will and not follow it is fruitless, but living out God's will makes it impossible not to worship. "When people diligently pursue God's will in everyday life, worshiping in church takes on a whole new dimension. When a farmer works hard in the field, he comes home hungry for dinner. For the Christian worker, plowing the field, planting the seed and taking in the harvest develops an appetite for God that is satisfied in worship" (Park, *To Know You More*, p. 57).

Question 9. There are many possible reasons people don't use their gifts: unawareness of what they do well, false modesty, distrust of God, selfishness, fear of failure, the desire to have a different gift, laziness or entanglement in distractions.

Question 10. One possible definition: "Real worship is the offering of everyday life to [God], not something transacted in a church, but something which sees the whole world as the temple of the living God" (William Barclay, *The Letter to the Romans*, rev. ed. [Philadelphia: Westminster Press, 1975], p. 157).

Study 8. Our Longing Fulfilled. Revelation 21:1-8.

Purpose: To embrace the vision we've been given in Revelation in order to keep our worship meaningful and alive.

Question 1. The promise in verse 6 hearkens back to our first study in Psalm 63. After a lifetime of thirsting after God, we will find satisfaction in a heaven and earth where God is present and all things have been made new. This free drink of life (Is 55:1; Jn 4:14) is a gift made possible by the sacrificial death of Jesus, as we saw in Mark 14 (see also Rom 5:15-19).

The promises in verse 4 are a reversal of Genesis 2:17 and 3:16-19, and are foretold in Isaiah 25:8; 35:10 and 65:19.

Question 2. From verse 1 it appears that the sea will pass away. In the Hebrew mindset the sea personified the power that fought against God and was thus feared. Its disappearance, therefore, could represent the ultimate triumph of God over evil and his enemies. On the flip side, God's words will not pass away (v. 5). These are just two possible answers to this question.

Question 3. God has always yearned for an intimate relationship with his people, like a marriage relationship. The covenants we learned about in Exodus 24, Psalm 50 and Mark 14 point to God's desire for exclusive and mutual commitment. In the New Jerusalem, this relationship will become a permanent and constant reality for those who dwell there.

Question 4. See King Solomon's astonishment at the prospect in 2 Chronicles 6:18. The marriage metaphor is continued in this verse as we hear that God will live with his people, like husband and wife. This is a return to the state of affairs before the Fall in Genesis 3—no longer will people hide from God or be banished from his presence. The "now" in verse 3 indicates that all previous prophecies of God dwelling with people (see question five) will be fulfilled at the time of this announcement.

Question 5. See Exodus 25:8; Leviticus 26:11-12; Ezekiel 37:27; 48:35; Zechariah 2:10. God's righteous concerns, which have become our own (Is 61), and the will of God that we have come to understand through our lives of worship (Rom 12) will prevail, because only God will be worshiped in our new home. Encourage people to talk specifically about injustices and wrongs in the world that will be righted by God's *new* order (v. 4).

Question 7. Alpha and Omega are the first and last letters of the Greek alphabet. These titles, which Jesus applies to himself in Revelation 22:13, signify that God rules over all of human history. "In the beginning God created the heavens and the earth" (Gen 1:1); in the end, God created the new heaven and new earth. In between, God sovereignly carried out every one of his purposes to redeem humankind.

Question 8. Unlike Jesus' followers and even Jesus himself, they have not overcome (see Rev 2:7, 11, 17, 26; 3:5, 12, 21). They have given in to the temptation to doubt or distrust God, or have outright rebelled against him (for example, those who practice magic arts are trying to have God's power without God). They probably think they have impunity, but they don't. Fire is a prominent image of punishment in both biblical and nonbiblical Jewish writings.

Question 9. You may want to ask people *why* it's easy or difficult for them to believe this vision is our future reality. Ideas for how to keep this picture front and center could include reading Scripture with an eye toward seeing messages about Christ's return and reign; painting a picture of this passage; singing more worship songs that celebrate heaven or asking God to make heaven more concrete. I also highly recommend the book *The Sacred Romance: Drawing Closer to the Heart of God* by Brent Curtis and John Eldredge (Thomas Nelson, 1997), which vividly captures what we have to look forward to.

Sundee Frazier is a full-time mother and children's writer. She worked for InterVarsity Christian Fellowship for ten years, first on campus staff and then as the worship leader with her husband, Matt, for Urbana 2000, InterVarsity's student missions convention. She is also the author of Check All That Apply: Finding Wholeness as a Multiracial Person *and* Brendan Buckley's Universe and Everything in It.